Baby Animals

Elizabeth Austen

2 bears

1 cub

2 otters

1 pup

2 horses

1 foal

2 kangaroos

1 joey

2 dogs

4 puppies

2 ducks

5 ducklings

2 hamsters

5 pups

2 pigs

9 piglets

Let's Do Science!

How are baby animals like their parents? Try this!

What to Get

- glue
- paper and pencil
- pictures of baby animals and parent animals
- scissors

What to Do

1. Make a chart like this one.

2. Glue pictures of parent animals in the *Parents* column. Glue pictures of baby animals in the *Babies* column.

3. How are the parents and their babies the same? How are they different?

Glossary

cub—a baby bear

foal—a baby horse

joey—a baby kangaroo

Index

Your Turn!

Go visit a real baby animal if you can. Or, find one in a book. How is the baby like its parents? How is it different?

Consultants

Sally Creel, Ed.D.
Curriculum Consultant

Leann Iacuone, M.A.T., NBCT, ATC
Riverside Unified School District

Jill Tobin
California Teacher of the Year
Semi-Finalist
Burbank Unified School District

Publishing Credits

Conni Medina, M.A.Ed., *Managing Editor*
Lee Aucoin, *Creative Director*
Diana Kenney, M.A.Ed., NBCT, *Senior Editor*
Lynette Tanner, *Editor*
Lexa Hoang, *Designer*
Hillary Dunlap, *Photo Editor*
Rachelle Cracchiolo, M.S.Ed., *Publisher*

Image Credits: p.15 Maximilian Weinzier/Alamy; p.16 Nikolai Tsvetkov/Dreamstime; p.4 iStock; pp.18–19 (illustrations) Rusty Kinnunen; all other images from Shutterstock.

Library of Congress Cataloging-in-Publication Data

Austen, Elizabeth (Elizabeth Charlotte), author.
Baby animals / Elizabeth Austen.
pages cm
Summary: "It is time to learn about animal babies."—Provided by publisher.
Audience: K to grade 3.
Includes index.
ISBN 978-1-4807-4521-6 (pbk.) —
ISBN 978-1-4807-5130-9 (ebook)
1. Animals—Infancy—Juvenile literature.
2. Counting—Juvenile literature. I. Title.
QK661.A95 2015
591.3'92—dc23

2014008607

Teacher Created Materials
5301 Oceanus Drive
Huntington Beach, CA 92649-1030
http://www.tcmpub.com

ISBN 978-1-4807-4521-6

Printed by: 590835
Printed in: China